Mastering a Manipulator through Spiritual Warfare

The Keys to Empowerment through

Alicia S. Coleman

Kingdom Builders Publications LLC

© 2019 Alicia S. Coleman
Mastering a Manipulator through Spiritual Warfare
Kingdom Builders Publications, LLC

All rights reserved. No part of this book may be reproduced or transmitted in any form or by any means without written permission from the author.

Printed in the USA

ISBN 978-0-578-54965-1 Soft Cover

Authored by
Alicia S. Coleman

Editor
Wanda Brown
Kingdom Builders Publications

Cover Design
Christopher Davis of Ascension Company
LoMar Designs (workbook)

Alicia Coleman
PROJECTS, LLC
est. 2010

This Book Belongs to

DEDICATION

I dedicate this piece to all women who have lost themselves while searching for love. I want you to know that whatever happened prior to reading this book was not your fault. However, whatever you choose after this knowledge, you are responsible for. God loves you no matter what you have done or been through. Do not allow your past to define you. Surrender it all to Jesus for His burdens are light. You can become a new creature today through a relationship with Jesus Christ.

"The LORD is close to the brokenhearted; he rescues those whose spirits are crushed."
Psalms 34:18 (NLT)

CONTENTS

	Dedication	iv
	Foreword	vi
	Preface	12
1	The Leech	15
2	The Pit	25
3	The Predator	37
4	The Vulture	50
5	Dying to be Loved	62
6	Let Love Find You	67
	Afterword	69
	Probing Questions	70
	About the Author	72

FOREWORD

For many years I have pondered how to use my life experiences and observations to empower the lives of women. I know that my life's journey is not in vain. I do not need a show of hands to know that women are seeking ways out of volatile relationships. There are numerous women trying to escape toxic relationships. Women want to know that they are not alone. My purpose is to let you know that you can make better decisions, love yourselves, and overcome toxic relationships. Thus, I decided to write my first book, **Mastering a Manipulator: A Relationship Guide.**

I was so excited about authoring a book that I made a lot of mistakes which caused me to create a product full of grammatical errors. However, I still stand behind the content shared in my first book. Despite it all, I know that my readers embarked upon a cutting-edge book that provided valuable information, in a simple and personal way.

While most relationship books focus on a target audience with a higher socioeconomic status, this book is different. I recognize that dysfunctional relationships cross every barrier — ethnic, social, and economic. The goal of **Mastering a Manipulator: A Relationship Guide**, was to educate and empower women to get out of emotionally, mentally, and physically abusive relationships.

This second book will delve deeper by providing Biblical insight through inspired revelation, led by the Holy Spirit. The mission of this book is to incite deliverance and restoration of the whole person. This book will expose satanic and demonic plots, plans, and attacks on people. This second book is real, raw and relevant. This book will also enlighten those who have been bewitched by a partner. It will also provide scriptures and prayer snippets in each chapter that I believe are essential tools that can help you overcome manipulation, intimidation, control, infidelity, abuse, and even death. **Mastering a Manipulator through Spiritual Warfare** tackles these issues in a simple yet serious and Biblically sound manner.

Unlike the first publication, the foundation of this book is shared from a more seasoned standpoint based on my spiritual growth. I value God's standpoint over the opinions of others. That is why I felt led to re-examine these issues so that God will be glorified, and His people edified. This book will encourage you to explore the circumstances in your life. You may ask, "What are the circumstances that opened me up to become a victim of abuse, and how can I overcome these circumstances and become victorious?" Yes, the answers are still inside of you! The good news is that Jesus Christ did and will destroy the works of the enemy! Jesus did it just for you!

The thing that governs our daily lives is choice. I believe strongly in choice and that our choices determine our future. God has given us free will to choose either those things that are good or bad for our lives. Perhaps, there will always be those who choose to ignore truth and stay in bondage. However, women who take heed and choose God's way will experience a peace that surpasses all understanding. My heart breaks for those who choose to override what their conscience speaks and ignore what is right because they are choosing to remain in bondage forever.

After publishing my first book in 2007, **Mastering a Manipulator: A Relationship Guide,** I had several men approach me, agreeing that the book exposed many of their motives and behaviors and they were not too happy about it. Others shared that were remorseful about how they were living. Surprisingly, a few even identified themselves with one or more of the personality profiles discussed in the previous book. For me, these shared comments are confirmation that the book was on point. In other words, if demons show you who they are, believe them! Combined with my witness of the miraculous power and saving grace of Jesus Christ, these confirmations substantiate my belief that this book is a change agent, if you choose to adhere to its instructions.

Luke 6: 18 (NLT) says, *"The Spirit of the Lord is upon me, for he has anointed me to bring Good News to the poor. He has sent me to proclaim that captives will be released, that the blind will see, that the oppressed will be set free, and that the time of the Lord's favor has come."*

It was a beautiful, yet peculiar autumn day in 2010 when I accepted the calling of God to minister the Gospel of Jesus Christ. The Lord had been dealing with me in so many supernatural ways, sometimes speaking to me all night long. I was overwhelmed by emotions and worried if I was competent enough to handle such a great responsibility. Prior to this, I had experienced the power of being filled with the Holy Ghost; the signs and wonders followed. I experienced an undeniable transformation that caused me to have encounters that the human mind could never understand.

What the Lord did in me was nothing short of a miracle. It is what I refer to as a quick work. He connected me with various ministers who not only confirmed the calling on my life but trusted the Holy Spirit in me. My journey has been amazing, as God has guided me into a place of maturity, solitude and submission.

The word of God, (Romans 8:28), has taught me that, *"All things work together for the good, of them who loves the Lord and who are called according to His purpose."* Not some things, but all things! For this, I rejoice! It lets me know that everything I have ever gone through, the pain, guilt, shame, and suffering was for a greater purpose. I was reared in a dysfunctional home. I am the oldest of four children and the only girl. I love my father, however, it's no secret that he was a philanderer and physically abusive to my mother. I was an eyewitness to many incidents that affected many areas of my life as I grew older. I struggled academically until about the tenth grade. As if I did not have enough on my young plate, life dealt me one of the biggest blows ever, my brother Calvin was killed in a car accident at the age of 12. His identical twin suffered a traumatic brain injury and has been battling mental illness ever since.

I made a declaration at age eight that I would not stay in a relationship with a man who hit me. Although, I have kept that promise to myself, I have had my share of heartbreaks. I have been lied to, cheated on, used and discarded like I was nothing. However, I refused to accept this treatment as God's best for me. I wanted more and I refused to settle. Not only did I want more for me, but for my children who were products of a promiscuous lifestyle and failed relationships. I learned that despite how they got here, they are products of God's great grace. He trusted me to be their mother. My prayer life changed and therefore, so did my mindset. When, I fell short and sinned, God immediately convicted me. I was no longer interested in meaningless relationships. When I saw the signs that my man did not desire marriage, family, and purposing God, I broke all ties. I have been married now for over ten years to someone whose love I do not have to question. I am confident that God can do the same for you. I have made some poor choices and I have made some major comebacks. I have been poor and living on public assistance as a single mother while putting myself through college. I have overcome a neurological disease called Guillain Barre' Syndrome, congestive heart failure and had my gallbladder removed. I have overcome spiritual warfare designed to keep me from doing the will of God. You have no idea the opposition I had to go through just to write this for you. Things happen and no one is exempt! I just made the choice to overcome! What about you?

We see abuse every day among the poor and the prominent; it even makes headlines as governors, millionaires, and athletes are caught cheating and beating on their spouses and girlfriends. There are also many untold stories of wives and girlfriends murdered in cold blood. There are missing person's cases where husbands are allegedly suspected of murder for hire schemes. What's behind these heinous acts? How did this begin? What were the signs?

Amazingly, I found scriptures that not only confirmed what my first book stated but also gave deeper insight. Therefore, we will be revisiting the characteristics, backgrounds, and methods of operation of the four types of manipulators; the leech, the pit, the predator and the vulture. If you are a male who is reading this book, I want to challenge you to seek deliverance and Christian counseling. Also, if you know someone with these traits, break the silence, the ***guy code*** is not a term of endearment but an alliance to Satan himself.

The following scripture impacted my thinking tremendously. It revealed to me the invisible forces that are responsible for wickedness and evil schemes. Allow me to share **Ephesians 6:12 (NLT)**, *"For we are not fighting against flesh and blood enemies, but against evil rulers and authorities of the unseen world, against mighty powers in this dark world, and against evil spirits in the heavenly places."* When I got this revelation, I no longer focused on the person but the source. As I conclude this forward, I want to make the following disclaimer. This book is not about male bashing. I am not a feminist! I merely want you to live your fullest life, free of depression and oppression. I want you to love yourself and walk in your divine purpose.

I pray that the scales are removed from your eyes so that your vision will be clear. I believe clear vision is only possible through Jesus Christ. If you are not saved ask Jesus to come into your heart. Repent of your sins and make Him your Lord and Savior.

PREFACE

I was lying in bed trying to go back to sleep when I heard these words in my spirit, "Womanizing, manipulation and control are forms of bewitchment!" I was astonished! I began to listen as the Holy Spirit revealed to me the connection between what I had already written and what I have learned through studying the Word of God and witnessed and discerned through manifestations and attacks of witchcraft. I was baffled because I never could have made the connection before due to intellectualism. In most cases, when people hear words like witchcraft, they picture an ugly old lady with a big pot boiling, but that is not what I will be referring to in this book. The truth is, witchcraft come in many ways. Some forms have become so common that they have been deemed social issues rather than spiritual attacks. The Bible states, *"I will not have you ignorant of Satan's devices," **2 Cor. 2:11**.* The reality of this revelation quickly began to sit in. I realize this can sound scary, but I want to assure you, as stated in ***2 Timothy 1:7***, *"God has not given us the spirit of fear, He give us power, love and a sound mind."* May the truth set you free!

You must understand that prayer is key! One cannot defeat the enemy without prayer and the Word of God; they build your spiritual muscles. I am speaking of strong prayers, not just spewing out random words. Prayer is communicating with God. It is the key to knowing Him, worshipping Him, and activating the authority He has given you. Prayer is also a strategic weapon against the enemy. It surely helps a lot when you know that God is real, and you trust His words. ***Mark 3:27 (ESV)*** says, *"But no one can enter a strong man's house and plunder his goods unless he first binds the strong man. Then indeed he may plunder* *his house.* "If you are in an abusive relationship, the message you are conveying to your partner is that you're his property/house. When you enter into a relationship you enter an agreement. That agreement gives that individual access and permission to your mind and your body if you engage in sexual acts. What binding does is it places spiritual handcuffs on the spirit operating through this individual. Therefore, you must bind him spiritually through prayer before attempting to strip him of his power and break free!

    You may experience a war between your spirit and flesh as you read this book. The information that will be presented to you is so life altering that you might begin to experience demonic opposition. This is a manifestation of the unseen world that can come in many forms such as confusion, resistance, denial or rationalization. However, I decree and declare, in Jesus' Holy name, that His light will shine on those dark areas in your life. I pray the spiritual fish-like scales will be removed from your eyes, and you will begin to walk in a level of wisdom and discernment that you have never experienced before. As you feel a tug of war going on between your flesh and your spirit, I challenge you to continue reading. The demonic opposition I referred to earlier can cause sleepiness and distractions.

Prayer

Father God,
I come to you in the name of Jesus Christ, your only begotten son. Lord, I activate the power and authority that you have given me over demons, unclean spirits and all manners of sickness. Lord, I thank you in advance for healing, deliverance, and restoration. I bind and rebuke the spirit of lying, manipulation, control, rejection, and rebellion, in the name of Jesus Christ of Nazareth. He is my Savior and my Lord, and no weapon formed against me shall prosper! Every Satanic plan, plot, and attack is cancelled right now, in the name of Jesus! I bind all spirits of witchcraft and divination operating in my life, in Jesus name. I release my will from anyone who seeks to control me and submit my will to you! Lord, I love you. Teach me how to love myself.
I bind and rebuke all spirits of confusion, stubbornness, and mind control, in your name Jesus. Cover me in your blood Jesus.

Amen.

THE LEECH
Chapter One

"The leech has two daughters: Give and Give..."
Proverbs 30:15 (ESV)

We fall in love with potential and not the person we see. We become immune to the dysfunction and addicted to what it could be. With clouded vision, we stumble into murky waters making us accessible to the leech then we have the audacity to call that being a good woman. Change can occur in the lives of these men, but it is not your assignment as a woman to change anyone. Women are naturally nurturers therefore; it is nearly impossible for them not to display this trait. It's easy for us to want to help everyone but it's not your responsibility to change anyone. Change is the outward manifestation of an inward transformation.

Growing up as the only girl with a lot of male relatives and male friends, I was afforded the opportunity to witness a host of men practicing womanizing behaviors in various ways. My response, in my earlier years, was to always be alert, on guard, and emotionless. Subconsciously, I began to develop defense mechanisms. For the record, I do not recommend becoming an emotionally detached individual because it opens your spirit to other forms of bondage and hinders you from experiencing true love and abundant joy.

Ladies, I want to challenge you to take a good look at yourself and examine your relationships, past and present. Take a personal inventory of what you have experienced in past relationships as well as any volatile or enabling behaviors you exhibited. Many will find that they keep dating the same kind of person, they just look different. You must realize that it's something about you that keeps attracting the same things. It is not easy to do a self-evaluation. It is much easier to focus on the many injustices life has dealt you. As you take inventory pay attention to your patterns and all interactions you had with men, even male relatives. Now, without further ado, let me present to you, the leech!

I am sure that when you think of a leech, you think of a slick, wormy, blood-thirsty parasite that lurks in rivers and attaches itself to its prey, sucking blood until satisfaction is reached. Leeches, like other parasites, will drain you of energy as you become its source for food. You generally do not hear of fatalities from leeching but I'm sure if any parasite remains undetected long enough the consequence will be dire. The same principal applies to men who leech. They will cling to you, use you of all your resources until they are either removed or take you for everything you have. In most cases, the leech will detach and look for another victim when you have nothing more to offer.

Leeches do not usually pose a physical threat of harm. Once they have been detected, you can detach them without fear of serious bodily injury. They usually just slither their way out just as they slithered their way in. In the case of relationships, a leech is a person who never has anything! He has made a profession of mooching off the income of naïve or emotionally vulnerable women. Their motto is, "It's better to receive than to give," (this is a characteristic of Satan twisting the Word of God). If you check into the past of the leech you will find patterns of inconsistencies, sketchy work history, and jumping in and out of relationships. He might say that his ex was always nagging him or wasn't there for him. Truth is, she was either no longer able to take care of him or spoke firmly about him not having a job.

Extremely cunning, like the serpent that deceived Eve in the garden, he will appear so sweet, caring and attentive. He may use a little flattery and charm to gain access but for the most part he comes off as the abandoned puppy you want to bring home. Let's be honest, flattery is a well-dressed lie, not a compliment! It is a form of manipulation. Do not undermine flattery. It has stolen the innocence of many young girls. You may even think to yourself, he's misunderstood, or he's down on his luck. A leech will give you all the things his money cannot buy, such as running your bath water, rubbing your feet, and, even cook your dinner. After all, women are always saying, "It's the little things that count!" Although, this is true there is always someone out there looking to exploit that truth. Those things may sound great but beware, he has a motive which includes getting shelter, food, clothing, and of course, sex! Plus, let's be honest, that water, soap and food he cooked all came at your expense.

His method of operation is through a seducing spirit, that's how he hooks you. He seeks out those who have what he needs and who have a nurturing nature. The women he dates must have their own car, house and means of income. In return, he will provide her with every manner of sexual experiences she will allow. He may not have accomplished completing a job application, resume or interview, because his forte is sex. He will appear passionate, and emotionally in tuned with an extremely high sex drive! He is one of those that even if you were not initially attracted to him, he could change your perception of him within one conversation. He is referred to as a charmer and smooth talker. You cannot trust his lips. His tongue is a weapon of mass destruction. When the Bible speaks against charmers, you will find the following other names listed also, mediums, wizards, sorcerers, all of which our creator Jehovah deems detestable and abominations.

He is a dream seller, in plain terms, a liar. In the beginning, He will have a logical reason for not being able to contribute financially. He might convince you that he is in the process of obtaining employment or waiting on a court settlement. Truth is he cannot keep a job. One of the saddest things I have found is that he is a spoiled mama's boys. He could be the self- entitled baby of the family, an only child or simply lazy. He might use this form of behavior as a weapon of vengeance after being deceived in a past relationship. His intuitive ability makes him dangerous in the sense that he knows exactly what you like and want to hear. A leech can carry a spirit of poverty, debt or lack, causing your destiny to be altered. He will drain your resources and dry up all your avenues of revenue! Ask yourself this question, "Is this worth losing my possessions and forfeiting my inheritance?"

A leech is a fraud and con artists. He can and will become conveniently emotional. He's forever having a sob story and will even cry to play on your emotional vulnerabilities. He never truly takes responsibility for actions but rather finds ways to distract you from knowing his true intentions. He will have you feeling so guilty that you even suggested that he pull his own weight. He will manipulate you into making a vow to never leave him, the key word is vow. When you make a vow to someone you automatically enter a spiritual marriage, bond or covenant. The only person you should vow to in this manner is God himself and your husband during a marriage ceremony. Marriage between a man and a woman is an example of a godly vow; a godly soul tie that brings the couple together, making them one. Never make vows with the ungodly. This combined with sexual intercourse (sin) gives the enemy legal rights to enter your body and soul. People do this out of ignorance all the time, unaware of the spiritual implications.

Have you ever slept with someone and it seemed like you just couldn't break away from him? You became obsessed, although you knew the feeling was not mutual? You dream about them, think about them all the time or even smell his cologne lingering when he isn't there? Whenever you see him you are drawn to him like a moth to a flame? No matter what you tell yourself, you can't stay away? Ungodly soul ties are bonds formed through sexual sins of fornication or adultery. Many do not want to fathom this fact because it's scary to think about, especially if you have been with several partners. Think about it! Why wouldn't sexual intercourse be the easiest ways to transfer unclean spirits when we know it can bring disease and even human life? Allow me to elaborate a bit further. Humans are created in three parts, body, soul, and spirit. The soul is where your mind, will, and emotions live. What happens is that your souls become knitted together or entangled and you become enslaved. That is why so many women cannot seem to break away from the grips of a man they know is no good for them. There is a form of magic that can take place during intercourse, leaving one spellbound, in a trance, or mesmerized by the sexual experience. In fact, a well-known rapper wrote a song that referred to his genitals as a, "magic stick," something to think about, right? Sex is not bad. Sex is God's design. He purposed it for marriage. The enemy just perverted it.

The anatomy of men and women are obviously different. Men project and release, they are givers. Women intercept and catch, we are receivers. Therefore, I believe women are usually more likely to form emotional attachments, even during casual sexual encounters. In most cases, the male is often dumb founded by her instant desire for them to become more. The transference of spirits is not to be taken lightly. Don't you know that when you have sex with him you are also having sex with all the folks, he has had sex with; even in the realm of the spirit. This act brings confusion, double mindedness and even a change in your countenance. Not only can your very countenance change but you may start to share their mannerisms; the way they say certain thing, their attitudes and/or beliefs. Have you ever heard the following statements? "We are starting to think alike," or "We are together so much we're starting to look alike!"

Listen, the devil doesn't have loyalty to anyone. He couldn't even be loyal to the Most-High God. Please do not expect the leech to be faithful. He will always have a backup plan. In fact, he may not be able to keep his other women in check so they will generally find a way to let you know that he is unfaithful. I must warn you that if you become pregnant by a leech, prepare to be a single parent. What I'm about to say may come as a shock to you but there is no need to contact your local child support division, it will only bring you more frustration. When you decide to sleep with a guy who will not work and have other children who he does not provide for, it is insane to expect anything more from him. He may use his mother or new girlfriend to give some assistance for the child every now and then but do not get your hopes up for much more. However, if you choose to put him on child support don't be surprised when he is $50,000 behind in child support.

Everybody at some point has experienced being used by another person. These people are opportunists so you should not allow guilt or shame to sit in. However, there are things within your character that you must address through Christ. These things are not always sin, they can also be strongholds. I will examine strongholds in another chapter. The scripture tells us that we should not give place to the devil (Ephesians 4:27). Here are some examples of things that can open the doors to the leech, lust, fornication, passivity, being naïve, impatience, poor judgment, impulsiveness and low self-esteem. I want to take this time affirm you, I ask that you internalize these words and speak them over yourself daily!

I am loved!
I am forgiven!
I am fearfully and wonderfully made!
I am a woman of virtue!
I have a sound mind!
My body is a temple of the Holy Spirit!
Greater is He that is within me than he that's in the world!
I can do all things through Christ who strengthens me!
I am destined for greatness!
I am blessed and highly favored by God!

In order to be set free from bondage you must believe in Him who can keep you from falling, Jesus Christ. You must also have faith that He can deliver you. It is in His name that we have the power and authority to address and cast out demons. Without faith, it is impossible to please God. Faith without works is dead. Now let's get to work! I have found that most women find themselves mentally stuck, believing that they must seek closure before ending a relationship. News flash, closure starts with closing your legs. You must repent of the sins you committed. You must verbally denounce any vow or commitment you made to the individual. You must renounce the soul tie verbally, stating the person's name. (I would do this for past sexual partners also.)

Example: I denounce all vows or commitments I made with_____, in the name of Jesus. I dissolve all ungodly covenant relationships I made, through the blood of Jesus Christ. I now, in the name of my Lord and Savior Jesus Christ, renounce the ungodly soul tie I made with _____ through fornication and any other forms of sin. I repent and receive forgiveness for any sin that has opened the door for any spirit to enter and operate in my life, In Jesus' name. Amen.

Last but definitely not least, if there are any objects/gifts that were given to you by the individual that can hold a soul tie in place you must get rid of them. This includes, but it not limited to, love letters, pornography videos or photos, flowers, cards, lingerie, and yes, even jewelry. If you are serious about wanting to be free of dysfunction, depression, lies, cheating, or abuse of any kind, you will do these things.

Holding on to these things can give the spirit a legal right to linger. You must get rid of any residue that could hold that soul tie in place. Think about a situation where a man and woman lived together and after a disagreement, she put him out. What is one of the many ways he tries to regain access? He leaves items such as clothing, toothbrush etc. Why? So, he can have a legitimate reason to comeback.

As we close this chapter, I want you to know that forgiveness is a must. It is important to the healing process that you forgive the individual who hurt and took advantage of you. Forgiveness is not weakness it's strength. The inability to forgive will only hinder you from becoming victorious over the situation. Forgiveness doesn't mean you should be the person's friend, but if you have a child with him it is essential that you be cordial unless there is reason to believe there is a physical danger. As, I like to say, act like you got some sense! You want to ensure that your child doesn't suffer because you two cannot be civil. God has greater plans for you!

Prayer

Lord, I come to you in praise and thanksgiving. Thank you for your love, grace and mercy. Thank you for exposing the plan of the enemy. Thank you for removing the scales from my eyes. You are my strength and my redeemer. Thank you for forgiving my sins.
Teach me your ways and baptize me with your spirit so, that I can better know your will for me.
Create in me a clean heart and renew a right spirit with in me. Help me to keep myself sacred until you release me into marriage. I rebuke debt, lack and poverty.
Lord, destroy every yoke and false burden in my life. In Jesus name, I pray this prayer. Amen

THE PIT
Chapter Two

"Beware of dogs..." Philippians 3:2 (KJV)

Girl, he's a dog!" Have you ever heard those words? I am sure the answer is yes. For as long as I have been alive, I've heard that phrase used to describe guys who mistreat women. Hmmm, I wonder where the phrase came from. It's no secret that all men came from women and many have sisters who they would protect. We must understand that a dog's loyalty is limited. Sure, they identify with their mother, sister or daughter's mistreatment, that's family. However, when it comes to their behavior toward women, they lack the ability to connect emotionally to their wrong doings. There is a spirit that is blocking or hindering them from connecting to the pain of their victims, deeming them inhumane. They are emotionally detached. Let's profile him!

The pit gets his name from the dog, the pit bull. Dogs are one of America's most popular and sought after pets. Dogs are great animals to own but there are dangers that owners should be aware of. The pit bull can be a dangerous breed of dog. They often are bred to fight, just for the sport of it. Dogs are often referred to as man's best friend. You can walk them, pet and feed them, even allow them to lick your face. However, one day without warning the dog could attack you. In other words, he can turn on you without just cause. People are somehow under the impress that the enemy plays fair. Why would he? This is a war and the last time I checked ambushes are permissible.

Have you ever just looked at a pit? They are beautiful, aren't they? Smooth fur, piercing eyes and a distinctive walk. The male counterpart is similar in nature, very attractive. Often deemed a pretty boy, he seems to have a swagger that draws women. He may have a lot of money, dress well and drive a fancy car. In the beginning, he will appear loyal and make you feel so secure. He will take you places and buy you things. All this is part of his plan to make you feel like you are the most important person in his life, causing you to disregard any red flags you may have noticed. Blinded by his, "too good to be true" persona, you throw all caution to the wind. I'm sure you are familiar with a situation like this. The mere fact that he is so desirable is alluring. Everyone wants him but he chose you and that gives you a sense of power.

You may be introduced to his family and friends. Some may even drop subtle hints of his true nature in your ears. Don't tell him what was said, just watch and pray. Always keep that little information compartmentalized. Just as he plans skillfully, you too, must think and plan wisely. If you have encountered the pit, he will plan to bring you to a state of submission - to his will. To be clear, there is nothing immoral about submitting to your spouse, for the Word says, "*Wives submit yourselves to your husband,*" **Ephesians 5: 22-23**. However, God does not want you to experience abuse at the hand of another. It is not His plan for your life. Therefore, you must choose your partner wisely.

You must develop a keen awareness of his doggish ways.

First, you should always discern his character before or during the dating process. Then identify if there is compatibility, spirituality, ambition to succeed financially, and family-oriented desires before giving him your heart. If you don't see these characteristics take a stance, pray diligently, and seek godly counsel. Never convince yourself that you can change a person. You can influence him by modeling right behaviors, but you should not seek to change a person. God gives us free will and doesn't force us to do anything. Don't disregard anything, red flags, abusive language, sarcasms, controlling commands, etc. The ultimate question that lurks in those who are victimized by the pit is, "Why?" Let's explore the making of the pit!

ADAPTATION OF A DOG

Mr. popular, prince charming, and lady killer are some other names that might be used to describe the dog. These terms are used to describe womanizers! While I don't pretend to have all the answers, I do know the God who does. The Lord revealed something to me that may sound insignificant to you but trust me in the realm of the spirit it is huge. Words have power! The Bible says that, life and death are in the power of the tongue. People speak words that curse. They do not realize the power that their words carry. The words that flow from the mouth can impact the very life of the soul, when these words are internalized. When words are formed, dispatched, and shaped, the process has begun. It can poison one's character and manifest in actions towards others. Women tend to self-blame. We beat ourselves up with the why's and how's. We take failed relationships personally, but the root of his behavior is deeper than you.

In my first explanation of why, I must get to the root of the problem that birth pits. I believe a deep seeded curse was sown into the lives of these men during childhood. We must be very careful about the things we say, especially those things we speak over our children. The Lord revealed something extremely powerful to me as I was praying about the origin of the pit. It literally blew my mind! He said, "They are sometimes, birthed through word curses!" Puzzled by what I heard, I asked Him for an example. He showed me in an open vision, a beautiful, chubby, curly haired baby boy smiling as he sat in a stroller. Then the Lord said, "Heartbreaker!" Immediately, I was both astonished and I was convicted! I cannot count how many times I have heard people speak this over their sons. We call them charmers. I have even heard people say, "He is going to have a lot of girls when he grows up." We use certain words as if they are terms of endearment, without understanding the true ramifications of these statements. These are curses not compliments! I believe the Lord was telling me that these trends must be broken. The many words our children hear shape their lives. They become what we decree over their little lives. The word of God tells us in ***Job 22:28*** *that, "we can decree a thing and it shall be established."* Think about that!

The enemy does not play fair! Satan will use your own words against you. He uses your very own tongue to cause a breach in the spirit. A breach is an opening, a hole that provides entry. Mothers of adult sons who exhibit womanizer behaviors often wonder why he behaves this way. My question is how can you expect for an apple tree to grow when you planted lemons with your words? There is a divine law referred to as sowing and reaping. **Galatians 6:7-9** says,

"Do not be deceived, God is not mocked, whatsoever you sow you shall reap." "Speak the word of God over your sons and daughters lives and you will grow great fathers, mothers, wives and husbands. Speak life not death! Do not kill their purpose with your mouth. If his dad was an absent father, alcoholic, or womanizer etc., do not reinforce generational curses by saying, "He is going be just like his father!" (We will explore generational curses later).

Do you know what a feral child is? A feral child is a child who has lived without having contact with humans. There have been cases of young children lost in the forest who were adopted by a family of animals such as wolves or monkeys. Other feral children were abused by guardians and kept in cages with pets. In these extreme cases, these children began to adapt to the behaviors of animals. In many cases they are unable to speak. They may howl and walk on their hands and feet. Now, let's look at this spiritually as it relates to the pit. We have explored how the seed of a word curse causes an opening for the pit to be conceived. However, for a seed to grow it must be planted and watered. Planted represents environment. Many young boys are impressionable. What they see in their environment fuels and helps shape their personal development. Many do not have present fathers or positive role models. Exposure to womanizing behaviors waters the seed.

Are you still asking yourself why? Why me? Let me assure you that you did nothing wrong! Many times, we are looking for surface answers to deeply rooted issues. The issue is in him not you! Men have been telling the truth about themselves for years, but women could not or would not listen. They say, "It's not you, it's me!" Never blame yourself for your partner's infidelity. Cheating is a character flaw, due to his lack of loyalty and self-control. His misguided, childish, self-serving attributes causes him to sabotage all potentially successful relationships. Playing fetch with hearts becomes his pastime!

The seed of womanizing was sown in his life, then, reinforced by the watering of his environment. His true identity was negated by the words spoken over him therefore, he adapted to dog tendencies. The reason he broke off the relationship so suddenly was because your value depreciated! I am sure some woman is saying, "What?" Allow me to break it down for you. If you have ever purchased a car you know that after a few years, its value has significantly decreased. When he first met you, he called a lot and was very attentive. You were the most beautiful woman he had ever seen, and he had to have you! Maybe you were a new face in town or gave him a challenge. Regardless of the situation, his mind was set on having you. After you had fallen helplessly in love with him, got pregnant or maybe even married him, in his mind you are forever tied to him. Again, in his mind, if you are forever tied to him you will never be able let him go. The challenge no longer exists therefore he leaves in search of the next conquest. He's a player!

It is not your fault that he cannot commit! This is just a character flaw in him. He gets bored quickly, and it does not matter who you are or what you do! This is something he needs deliverance from. You need to take responsibility for what you can control. Ladies never make a man your god. This is idolatry! Statements like, "I worship the ground he walks on," should never be spoken! ***Matthew 7:6 (KJV)*** *says, "Give not that which is holy unto the dogs, neither cast ye your pearls* *before swine, lest they trample them under their feet, and turn again and rend you."* In this context, this verse is saying do not give your heart, mind and soul to a dog. Do not give your body to a pig because they will make you a door mat, then after walking all over you, they will turn and attack you! Never, deceive yourself into believing that you can lead your boyfriend to Christ while engaging in sexual sin with him.

Let's further consider the characteristics of the pit. What most women find disturbing is his calculated nature. He is one who will spoil you with his time and attention, making sure that you fall in love with him. He is the kind of guy, who after proposing, and planning a family with you, will get bored and leave without warning. He only marries the one who is most challenging. Pits love a challenge! If he knows that the only way he can really get his grips into you is by marrying you, he might do that. Hunting is a part of canine instincts and so is burying his bones. Another possible explanation for pit-like behavior is past heartbreaks and the inability to forgive. It could have happened in grade school, but he still struggles with forgiveness and will not easily allow himself to become emotionally vulnerable to anyone. This unresolved pain can also water the seeds planted through word curses.

INSPECT THE FRUIT

I don't want women to develop a spirit of paranoia or suspicion. Those spirits

BEFORE YOU EXPECT IT, YOU NEED TO INSPECT IT!

are not of God, in fact they are counterfeits! Discernment is a gift of the Holy Spirit in which those spirits mimic. Therefore, it is important to be baptized with the Holy Spirit. If you allow paranoia or suspicion to lead you instead of the Holy Spirit, when you do meet the right person your carnal mind might tell you, "Girl, he's a pit," when he's really not. Therefore, we must study the Word of God. The Bible tells us in Matthew 7:16, "You will know them by their fruit." The fruits of the pit are haughtiness, full of pride, arrogance and greed. Yes, he is cocky, big-headed, vain, boastful and materialistic. In the past I said the most annoying thing about the pit is that there are no warning signs, so it's hard to test him. What I meant by that is there are no warning signs of when he will turn your world upside down. One day you can be planning your future and the next day he might say, "I don't want you anymore!" The best way to prevent from becoming his victim is to be a fruit inspector. Trust your intuition and investigate by asking the correct questions. Most times, women do not know who they are dating because they fail to ask the correct questions. Ask about his past relationships and patterns of behaviors. Pay attention to what his family and friends say and if you sense that he is a pit, RUN! A promiscuous man is no more appealing than a promiscuous woman. There are no double standards in God's kingdom. Double standards indicate double mindedness. There is nothing cute about dating a man who thinks he is God's gift to all women. *Isaiah 56: 11 (NLT) says, "Like greedy dogs, they are never satisfied."*

    A pit is a conceited, self-centered cheater. You will wonder where he found the time to cheat because he is always with you. He is so suave that he can convince the other woman to keep a low profile in your presence. Truthfully, you may never find out that you weren't his only one until he wants you to know or the Lord snatches back the covers on his deceitfulness. There is no true remorse for his actions in fact he may even be vicious enough to taunt you with his new prize. However, there is one thing for sure, she won't have him long either. A pit rarely commits to one woman because getting the attention of beautiful women is what he thrives on. If you study the Bible you will find that before Satan became a fallen angel, he was a beautiful angel named Lucifer. Do not be blinded by what you see.

If you are wondering how I came up with the name pit, it is because they share three strong characteristics. Here is what to look for:

- *They are competitive*
- *They are territorial therefore many of them father children with different women*
- *They love to have sex*

MIND GAMES

Ladies who date, marry or have children with a pit may develop depression, low self-esteem and suicidal thoughts. He toys with the emotions of his women so much until it's like being on an emotional rollercoaster. One day he might say, "Baby, I love you." The next day he might say, "Find yourself another man." The Pit likes to play a lot of mental games! Meanwhile, his victims are left asking why? They begin to study themselves for any physical flaws that lead him to leave. They often ask themselves the following questions:

"Am I too fat or too skinny?"
"Did I nag him too much?"
"Did I please him?"

His victims may develop faulty thinking patterns based on strongholds, lies and deception. Strongholds cause you to view yourself and God incorrectly. They are designed to block you from God's best for your life. This is all a part of the enemy's plan.

In addition, I want to add that if you beat him at his own game by getting away before he releases you, victory you shall obtain. Your escape may seem daunting initially, but in time you will be forever grateful and hopefully warn others. He will become very upset. He may even speak words he knows will break you down, causing you and give in to his request of mending the relationship. Do not fall for it! Generally, he is not the type to invoke physical harm because you left. This guy is often too stuck on himself to allow you to see defeat. Instead he will ring your phone off the hook, persuade you with gifts and basically pursue you with a vengeance.

He will do these things secretly because he has an image to uphold. If you refuse to take him back, he'll respect you more. He will realize that he has bitten off more than he can chew. This along with prayer is the only way that you can help him realize that his behavior is not acceptable. On the contrary, however, if you fall back into his trap prepare for revenge. This time he will not be satisfied until you're completely devastated. I want you to be encouraged. You must stand strong. Dogs can sense weakness. Do not beat yourself up with the why and how questions. Instead, encourage yourself in the Lord.

I am the head, not the tail!
I am above, not beneath!
I am a virtuous woman. My worth is far above rubies!
I overcome evil with good!
I am seated in heavenly place with Christ.
I am saved!
I am redeemed!
I am a friend of God.
All of my needs are met according to His riches and glory
I am the woman of wisdom.
What the enemy meant for evil, God has turned it around for my good!

Prayer

> Lord God,
> I thank you for the spirit of truth and for bringing me out of darkness and into your marvelous light. I am eternally grateful for your unmerited favor in my life. Thank you, Lord, for making me a blessing so that I can be a blessing. I forgive any person who has ever hurt me, disappointed me, mistreated me, or rejected me, in the name of Jesus. I will put no other god before you, Lord. Cleanse me from all idols. I renounce all ungodly soul ties and immoral relationships, in the name of Jesus. I receive deliverance through the blood of Jesus. I renounce all hatred, anger, resentment, revenge, retaliation, unforgiving, and bitterness, in the name of Jesus. I renounce all ungodly thought patterns and belief systems, in the name of Jesus. I break all spoken curses and negative words that I have spoken over my life and the lives of others, in the name of Jesus. I even, break all spoken curses and negative words spoken over my life by others, in Jesus name I pray. Amen!

Note: If you are married to him, I am in no way advising you to divorce. That is something you must seek God on.

THE PREDATOR
Chapter Three

"...your adversary the devil, as a roaring lion, walks about, seeking whom he may devour." 1 Peter 5:8 (KJV)

Have you ever watched the National Geographic or Discovery channel? Did you secretly wonder, "How in the world a huge elephant would allow a tiger to devour it? I mean, there is an obvious difference in their size. Well, I often wonder the same thing when I see strong, intelligent women fall victim to the guy I like to call the predator. The word predator is pretty much self-explanatory. Generally, he is thought of as an animal whose sole purpose or survival depends upon preying on other animals. However, we know that an animal's instinctive nature is not limited to the animal kingdom. You may be envisioning a swift and fearless animal stalking its prey, watching carefully, studying every move, waiting for the precise moment to attack. You may even envision animals using special techniques to overpower the victim, ripping it to shreds with teeth and claws.

Predators are aggressive and domineering species. A true predator will not choose a random target he is much more calculated and sinister. Tigers and eagles are known for their keen vision! A tiger will watch and wait. It gets close and plans its attack. A shark will also watch and wait. I've seen movies about how they intimidate their victims by circling them. This is true of human predators as well. The human predator feeds off his prey. The desire is to conquer her and make her subservient, (this feeds his ego and his need to be wanted). He is not attracted to underachieving women or those who lack ambition because that would be too easy. Rather, he is intrigued by independent thinking, hard working women. Those he typically pursues are college students, teachers, nurses and other professional women. Like a moth to a flame, he is drawn in by her confidence, drive and tenacity. Her ability to resist his initial advances stimulates him. He secretly perceives this as cockiness so he desires to bring her down a notch or two. It reminds me of the scripture where Jesus says to Peter, *"Simon, Satan desires to have you that he may sift you as wheat."* **Luke 22:31**

Of course, in the beginning he was a dream. He was attentive, thoughtful and caring. Unlike most men, he is very detail oriented. He remembers the day he first met you in the park, it was spring. You wore your hair in a bun with a white flower on the side. Your dress was lavender, and you were with your cousin, April, playing spades on a checkered blanket under the tree. He listens to you as you reveal your innermost feelings, doubts, insecurities, and past experiences. Without your knowledge, he is studying you and taking inventory. All these could be great attributes, if only his motives were good.

I was blown away when the Holy Spirit spoke to me and said, "A reversed Delilah!" There is a story in the Bible about a powerful warrior named Samson who fell in love with a beautiful woman named Delilah, who was assigned to help destroy him! Her mission was to learn the secret that made him such a mighty, undefeated warrior. God had given him supernatural strength with instructions that his hair should never be cut in order for him to remain victorious. Delilah knew very well how to entice men; she was like a special agent. She seduced Samson and questioned him daily about what made him so strong. At first, he lied but she kept pressing and manipulating him until finally, he poured out his heart and told her that his strength was in his hair. As he slept, she called for a man to cut off seven locks of his hair. Samson lost his strength and then she turned him over to his enemies.

The predator operates a little different. He doesn't want to know your strengths he wants to know your weaknesses. He gets you to open up to him and then he uses your weaknesses against you. Have you ever dated someone who used the very things you revealed to them in confidence, against you? That is true betrayal! There is a great Tyler Perry movie called *Temptation: Confessions of a Marriage Counselor* that has a very accurate depiction of the predator. In this movie, a beautiful young woman named Judith, who wanted to become a marriage counselor, met Harley, a very aggressive, charming, and rich young man. Judith was not looking for trouble; she was married to a handsome, humble man named Brice who she'd known since childhood. She grew up in a strong Christian home and lived a plain life. Her husband loved her, but he began to take her grant. He failed to make her feel protected, and he forgot her birthday two years in a row. Harley began to pursue her relentlessly, by coming to her job frequently, giving her compliments, being observant and attentive to her, sending her flowers on her birthday, etc. He became a student of Judith, meaning he studied her! He intrigued her and stirred something in her that she didn't realize was there. She tried to fight his advances, but she was inexperienced with charmers, and secretly began to look forward to the attention. She didn't realize that she was playing with fire. She never thought she would find herself in an adulterous relationship until the business trip! The movie doesn't show this, but it became apparent that Judith experienced something sexual with Harley that hooked her! Suddenly, she was drinking, snorting cocaine with him, leaving home in the middle of the night to be with him, and disrespecting her mother and husband. She wanted a divorce! After he charmed her, he became physically abusive and gave her HIV. It was apparent as I watched this movie that Harley fit the profile of the predator!

The predator is a wolf in sheep's clothing, ears up like antennas and eyes focused, looking for any flaws or insecurities he can exploit. Imagine that you are in a safari in Africa and you see a herd of gazelles. One of them is nursing a nasty wound on its hind leg. Who will the lioness most likely target for food to feed her young? This wound has made the gazelle an easy target. This is how the predator disarms and enslaves his women. For example, maybe you're overweight, have an absent father or were promiscuous in the past. In the case of Judith, she was naïve, lacking spontaneity and attention from her husband.

During disagreements, the predator will use information you shared with him as ammunition to attack your self-esteem. It is heart wrecking to discover that the person who said he loves you turns on you and use your insecurities as fiery darts. He says he's sorry when you confront him but continues to make sly remarks over the course of the relationship. This is not a sign of a remorseful individual.

As a licensed social worker, I know many of these men have serious issues with women because of their own childhood trauma. Their issue may be a result of having a domineering mother, abandonment issues, rejection from girls during adolescence, etc. Whether it's a life issue or a generational curse, the predator has deeply seeded bitterness, resentment and hatred towards females.

Predators use control tactics as a tool to dominate. Physical abuse doesn't usually occur at the beginning of the relationship, but if you wait around long enough it's coming! We can learn a lot by watching animals. In the animal kingdom, they stay in herds to combat attacks.

When an individual is isolated or does not tell others what is happening she becomes more defenseless. Predators know that you are stronger in numbers. One of the first tactics the predator will use is isolation, by taking the victim away from friends and family. Once you allow him to dictate where you go, who you hang around, and what you wear, he knows that he has gained control. I am not speaking of healthy compromises and mutual respect, there is a difference. You can alter your entire lifestyle to gain his approval but it's never enough. If you make all the changes he demands, there will come a time when you no longer recognize yourself. Your identity has been stolen!

Predators are destiny robbers. They thrive on killing hopes and dreams. This is confirmed through the inspired Word of God, "The thief comes for to steal, and to kill and to destroy..." (John 10:10). What I found so powerful about this verse is that it doesn't say to steal or to kill or to destroy, it says all three! He knows that if he can control your mind then he can control your body and ultimately your soul. When the predator takes control of your mind, he fills it with lies like

those below:
> *No one will love you like I do!*
> *People are jealous of our relationship!*
> *All the other men just want you for sex!*

Some of you might be saying mind control is not true but the predator will convince you to believe what he says.

I can identify with this personally. I dated a predator in college. He started out being mostly verbally abusive which advanced to him being physically abusive, even in public. He'd call me derogatory names. He cheated on me often, while convincing me that he rescued me from a life of whoring. I knew it wasn't true but since I was no angel, I began to question myself. I was confused. I remember when I first started trying to read the Bible he would hide it from me. When the physical abuse began, I questioned how I could allow this to happen to me? It was never a fair fight because I never hit him back and that was not me. I was known to be very strong, assertive and confident! I never took anything off anyone! However, he caught me during a very vulnerable time in my life. I was a single parent raising my son alone and struggling in every area of my life. I felt I had no other choice but to stay, despite how miserable I was in the relationship. When I think back on that situation I think of a segment of **Galatians 3:1** that says, *"...who has bewitched you?"*

For me, it was the predator that bewitched me and convinced me to go against what I knew to be right! I could not even think for myself. I know now that was not the will of my Heavenly Father.

If this is you, it has now probably escalated to a point that any sign of independent thinking has made you a target for verbal and physical threats. Any attempt to break away results in violence. An angry predator will literally stomp your light out! He must instill fear in you. He will not see your desire for freedom as something he caused. Instead, he becomes an accuser, blaming you for wanting to leave because you are seeing another man. He is extremely jealous! Again, the Bible has already exposed him of this very thing. Revelations 12:10 describes him as, "...the accuser of the brethren which accused them before our God day and night..." Yes, you read it correctly day and night! He constantly accuses the victim of cheating when it's really him.

In my case, the predator got a girl pregnant while dating me and lied about it. I later discovered that he even drove my car to see her. One day she showed up on campus, so pregnant that she looked like she was about to burst! She said, "Hey, Z," to my then one-year-old son! That's how I found out that the predator had taken my son around her. My mouth dropped but I didn't say a word because by that time, I had already received my breakthrough!

In any toxic relationship, there are levels! It is important to take note of any indicators of violent tendencies. The following predicators of toxicity are important to understanding violent attributes. The term toxicity refers to the degree by which a matter can harm humans. The leech usually falls under acute toxicity which does not have lasting effects after removal of exposure. The pit falls under the category of sub-chronic toxicity which is the ability of a toxic substance to cause effects for more than one year but less than the lifetime of the exposed organism. However, the predator and the vulture are more severe. They fall under the chronic toxicity category. They have the ability to cause harmful effects over an extended period of time. Repeated or continuous exposure can sometimes last for the entire life or result in death. Since you now have a better understanding of the seriousness of a toxic relationship it is time to encourage yourself to stay aware, stay empowered, and always closed minded toward toxic substances. It is crucial that you not invite nor accept toxicity to have a seat in your relationship. When or if you are exposed to behaviors that affect your emotional, spiritual, mental or physical well-being, RUN for your life! God loves you and does not intend for you to encounter such unfavorable circumstances.

It is important to always use discernment. This is a gift of the spirit that God has given us to detect and prevent us from being deceived by evil spirits. As a child, I was exposed to domestic violence in my home. Therefore, I was always keen on discerning the signs of an abuser. When I encountered guys who were extremely clingy, possessive or overly authoritative, I would find the first exit and never return.

Just in case you're wondering how I got out of that relationship in college, SPRING BREAK! He lived in another state and went home for spring break and I had seven days to break that bad habit. I started praying, became my own motivational speaker, and ignored his phone calls! Guess what? I GOT MY BREAKTHROUGH! Praise God! I want to also add that God doesn't want us to be taken advantage of that is why He will not have us ignorant of Satan's schemes, **(2 Corinthians 10-11)**. If you do not have strong discernment, pray for it. Always seek God before making any decisions and trust what He places in your spirit. God will never mislead you. He is not a man, He cannot lie! Affirm yourself with truth.

> *I am complete in Christ!*
> *I have the mind of Christ! God supplies all my needs!*
> *I walk in abundant blessings! I was created with a purpose!*
> *I overcome evil with good!*
> *I will live a purpose driven life.*
> *I have power to tread on serpents and scorpions! I am rooted and grounded in love!*
> *I bear good fruit!*
> *I have boldness and access in Christ!*
> *I have been chosen by Christ before the foundation of the world was formed!*

Presented next are two stories which provide relatable illustrations. Please do not get confused to think that it will be 100% accurate to your situation. In the field of mental health counseling, the DSM-V Manual is used to determine diagnosis for mental illness. It may give eight characteristics, but it only takes four to five of those to meet the criteria for diagnosis. It's the same with this book. It is possible to show signs of two or more of the manipulators dissected in this book, but these are the ones I like to call mutts (a mixed dog with no definable type of breed). Make no mistake these are demonic spirits. The thing you must know about demonic spirits is that they group according to their nature and there is a strongman (a ruling spirit) in charge. They are like a family. By grouping these evil spirits together, they get stronger. In both situations, you can see how generational curses are passed along. In this case you foresee that Cindy will mostly like become a victim of domestic violence and sexual exploitation. *This piece was created by my son Zaire Matthews who is the rapper of the family.*

> Let me tell you a story about girl name Cindy
> She was a college girl that was new to the city
> Wasn't looking for a dude, she was independent
> Was on top of her classes, baby was really getting in
> Never had her father because her daddy was a prison
> Never loved by a man because of his decision.
> He used to beat her mother because of his suspicion.
> Thought she was cheating but in reality, she didn't.
> She grew up hating men and started dating women
> Until she met a dude on campus name Dillon
> At first, they started of texting and then it went to chilling
> Fell in love with his ways but never knew he was pimping
> She was blinded by the fact that Dillon actually pursued
> But he really chose her, just to use her.
> One day she decided to seduce her
> First time having sex, so it blew her…

Our second story leads with Megan who is 25 years old and struggles with low self-esteem. She was seen in the local hospital after an apparent overdose from a combination of prescription drugs and alcohol. She has been in and out of toxic relationships. She is never content with being single.

She never met her father; she just knows that his name is Matthew. All she ever heard about him was that he was no good and left her mother, Tonya, after finding out she was pregnant. Megan's mother was young and could not properly care for the baby therefore she left her with her grandmother. When Megan was eleven years old she was molested by her uncle. When she told her grandmother, she was called a liar. Her Grandmother repeatedly told her that she was just like her no-good mother and father. Meagan longed for a relationship with her mother, but Tonya was too focused on her new boyfriend.

Megan felt rejected by her parents and her grandmother. By the time she entered middle school she became increasingly defiant and rebellious. Her grandmother decided it was too much for her and sent her to a home for troubled teens. Megan said to herself, "No one will ever hurt me again. I will never trust anyone else." She struggled to make friends and would lash out at others. When asked about her hopes and dreams she would respond, "I don't care!" Megan would often isolate herself from others and lost interest in doing things. In high school, Megan started engaging in sex to numb her pain. She dropped out of school after becoming pregnant. It seemed history was repeating itself. Her child's father broke up with her and denied paternity.

When Megan gave birth to her son, Ryan, her mother Tonya came back into her life. They, however, started having arguments. Tonya accused Megan of flirting with the guys she dated. Their arguments got so bad that the authorities were called in to mediate. At age 21, Megan decided that she would never speak to her mother again. Shortly, afterwards she got pregnant with her second child by her friend with benefits. After having her daughter, she started drinking heavily and abusing prescription drugs.

Mastering a Manipulator through Spiritual Warfare

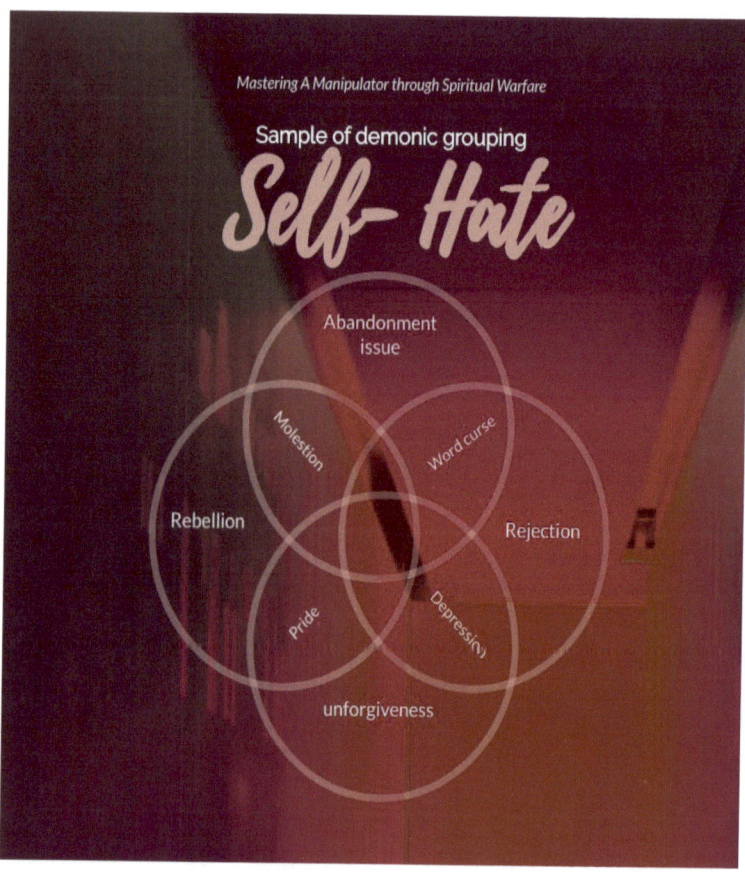

Now that you have been educated on the predator and how he operates, let's pray for deliverance and restoration, in Jesus name!

Prayer

Father God,

I thank you for your divine protection. I thank you for being a present help in times of trouble. I thank you that when the enemy comes in like a flood you will lift up a standard against him. I thank you that no weapon formed against me shall prosper. I loose myself of all relationships based on control, domination, or manipulation, in the name of Jesus. I bind and loose myself of all spirits of mind control, confusion, bondage, sorcery and witchcraft, in Jesus name! I rebuke all spirits that are hindering and blocking your will for my life. The blood of Jesus is against all principalities, powers, wickedness and rulers operating in my life. I close up any breach in my life that would give Satan and demons access, in Jesus name. I repent of all sin and ask you to forgive me. I rebuke all seducing spirits that would come my way. Hide me O, Lord, from my enemies. Break every assignment of death off my life, in the name of Jesus. Amen!

THE VULTURE
Chapter Four

"Wherever the corpse is, there the vultures will gather." Matthew 24:28 (ESV)

A U.S. Justice Department study shows that two-thirds of violent attacks against women are committed by someone they know. In the United States, one of the most dangerous places for a woman is sometimes in her own home. Approximately 1,500 women are killed each year by their partner. The question many ask is, "Why didn't she leave?" This is not a surface issue therefore we cannot expect a superficial answer. The same reason she stays is the same reason he abuses. The answer is demonic oppression. How does one become demonically oppressed? I understand speaking of demons is a taboo subject in this country and that it is preferred that a psychological assessment be made for certain behaviors. Even those of the Christian faith who know that Jesus spent a great deal of time casting out evil spirits, find a diagnosis of bipolar disorder somehow easier to cope with. The cause is almost always ruled as mental illness and a pill to subdue the individual is given but no one ever gets healed, only treated!

A vulture is described as a kind of bird or fowl that preys on injured or rotting flesh. This fowl is described in the Old Testament as a detestable creature. You can find these scavengers circling a corpse or even an injured animal. Often referred to as buzzards, I have seen them dismember roadkill in a short period. I find them to be the dirtiest, most appalling creatures on this earth. They do not have eagle vision, but they have a keen sense of smell. When I think of humans with vulture characteristics, I am reminded of this old song I heard in church when I was little. The chorus goes like this, "It's just like pouring water on a drowning man." The vulture pretends he means well when in fact, he is not concerned about helping hurting women. It is all a ploy, a sick satanic scheme to get what he can get out of an already lifeless situation. Vultures are not just opportunists, they are exploiters!

When I had my oldest son, I was a single parent. I moved into a Section 8 apartment while completing my college education. Believe it or not, human vultures seemed to circle that complex day and night in their luxury cars. I briefly encountered one on my twenty-second birthday. I was on my way to check my mail when he suddenly drove up to me in his shiny gray Mercedes. He seemed to be too good to be true and he was. He complimented me and I told him it was my birthday. Instantly, he handed me a fifty-dollar bill along with his business card. He told me to call him sometimes but said if his wife answered the phone to tell her that I was calling for business purposes. Although, I was a piece of work back them, I had a conscience! Therefore, I threw his number in the dumpster and enjoyed the extra cash. They came often patrolling the complex, looking for a cheap thrill. In poverty-stricken areas you will find a survival of the fittest mentality. These exploiters know young, single parents, addicts or runaways will do whatever it takes to survive. The vultures are more than willing to make her sell her soul for forty bucks.

I have known people who were sexually and physically abused countless times by different people. I use to wonder how these people always seemed to find them. It seemed like there was a magnetic pull that drew these scoundrels to them. I believe they have an innate ability from demonic forces that detects hurt, despair, insecurities and hopelessness. Those of the New Thought Movement might say it's the law of attraction. Many celebrities follow this movement. After doing some research, I discovered that the law of attraction is nothing more than sorcery (witchcraft). The vulture is dispatched to people with issues. He has counterfeit discernment therefore he can sense despair, hopelessness, rejection or loneliness and smells fear in women. I have discovered that vultures mostly prey on women who are uneducated, unemployed or a single parent, have been neglected or abused, who have little family support, or suffer from illness. It doesn't matter what the situation is, he can sense if she is in a vulnerable state. Just like a predator, wherever you find the wounded you will find him circling its prey, sniffing out the stench of hopelessness and despair. He knows that she is on a quest to find love and that she has not grasped the fact that what she really needs is God because He is love. She has never experienced a healthy display of love so lust can easily masquerade in its place!

The vulture presents himself as a knight in shining armor just like his father Satan, who disguises himself as an angel of light (**2 Corinthians 11:14**). The key word, disguises, lets us know that he is not authentic. Within a short period, he is already professing his love for you. He swears that he will never treat you differently because of what you have been through; strongly suggesting that he is not like other guys. You feel obligated to say you love him too. To have someone to love you when you don't even love yourself, will make you feel that you should be grateful. He is always emphasizing that he has your best interest at heart so that when things get ugly you will blame yourself saying, "It's not his fault!" Allow me to explain to you what love does and what love is not. First, Love should NOT suffocate! Suffocation kills! It kills your TRUE identity! It kills your purpose and destiny! Suffocation controls! It makes you feel obligated, causing you to feel false guilt and burdens! It makes you a people pleaser! It becomes Idolatry! Love is NOT a weapon! You should NOT feel that you will lose it if you say NO! That kind of love is NOT of God, it is a COUNTERFEIT!

DON'T LOVE ME TO DEATH!

For my skeptics who are saying, "Where is she getting the counterfeit stuff from?" Let me help you. God is love! First John 4: 8 says, "He who does not love does not know God, for God is love." Also, **1 Corinthians 13:4-7,** says, *"Love is patient, love is kind. It does not envy, it does not boast, it is not proud. It does not dishonor others, it is not self-seeking, it is not easily angered, and it keeps no record of wrongs. Love does not delight in evil but rejoices with the truth. It always protects, always trusts, always hopes, and always perseveres."*

Lucifer was an angel who tried to exalt himself over God and got kicked out of Heaven. We know to counterfeit means to copy, duplicate or imitate! Therefore, when you see the words ***as*** or ***like*** that is an indicator of an imposter!

LOOK AT THIS!

> *"How you are fallen from heaven, O Lucifer, son of the morning! How you are cut down to the ground, you who weakened the nations! For you have said in your heart: 'I will ascend into heaven; I will exalt my throne above the stars of God; I will also sit on the mount of the congregation on the farthest sides of the north; I will ascend above the heights of the clouds, I will be like the Most High.'"*
>
> *Isaiah 14:12-14*

That passage is proof that Satan, the imposter, wants to deceive others into believing that He can be God.

A vulture is swift and strong. He starts the abuse very early in the relationship. He only dates women with low self-esteem. This male chauvinist is quick to taunt his victim with degrading words and profanities. He enjoys belittling her because it makes him feel big; after all he has his own insecurities to cover up. Although he has an evil spirit that is controlling, he is also very needy. He wants her to believe that she needs him, but in actuality he needs her to validate his manhood. There are different types of vultures, but they are all dangerous.

One of the most vulnerable times that women can meet vultures is after leaving a bad relationship. Therefore, it is important to take time off from dating when getting out of a relationship. Use the down time to work on your goals and to improve your quality of life. Take the time to realize your value. Do not rush into another relationship, trying to fill a void with a man. Instead, fill that void with God!

Jesus Christ makes me whole! I present my body as a living sacrifice. No weapon formed against me will prosper. I am blessed going in and coming out! I will live and not die, and I will proclaim the name of the Lord!!

Sometimes a vulture is called a male chauvinist, because he taunts women in many demeaning ways. A vulture can be so deranged that he will beat a woman, and then have her apologize for pushing him that far. He might feel that he has the right to cheat but if she even says hello to the mailman there is a problem. He might say that if he didn't love her so much, he wouldn't get so angry. Please do not be deceived, if he beat his previous girlfriend, he will do the same to y

A vulture has the potential to kill. If he has wealth, don't be impressed because he is no different, in fact, he just has more ammunition. He is the type who threatens, "If you leave, you leave with nothing, and that includes the children!" He might also threaten to kill you, himself, the children or anyone he *thinks* you're dating. A vulture is emotionally unstable and the hardest to get rid of. Finding inner strength and escaping his traps are mandatory! If you have children, you must get them out immediately!

You may be surprised but a vulture can start displaying signs of predatory behavior in the early teen years. Many teenage girls are secretly being abused by their boyfriends. There is never a justifiable reason for a man to fight a woman.

Personally, I feel that anyone who feels comfortable being your daddy and your man should not be trusted. There is nothing normal about a man chastising you like he's your father, and then when night falls, he climbs into bed with you to have sex. That is an extremely perverse spirit!

A vulture can be a malicious person. Have you ever wondered what kind of person would introduce his girlfriend to cocaine or prostitution? A vulture! What kind of human being would convince his girlfriend to traffic drugs with or for him, and put the charges on her when they get caught? A vulture! What kind of individual forces his girlfriend to bring another woman in the bed? A vulture! What type of person would rape his girlfriend's daughter and convince her that the child is a liar? Yes, a vulture! I urge you to be careful who you allow around your child. Do not get so caught up in your own need to feel loved that you jeopardize your child's life! Your child deserves the chances you may have never received!

Ladies beware of any generational curses or iniquities that could shape your personality in a way that will cause you to seek dysfunctional relationships. Generational curses are issues that are profound in families and resurface from generation to generation (examples of generational curses are addictions, poverty, domestic violence, incest, suicide and murder). Have you ever heard statements like, "I feel like he doesn't love me if he doesn't hit me," or "It's my fault!" To most people this sounds insane but for someone who has never witnessed an authentic display of love, this is life! Have you ever been raped? Are you homeless? Did you have your father in the home? Do you struggle with addictions? Have you been abused or abandoned? These situations are not hopeless. Break the cycle before it attacks your future generations. These issues are deeply rooted. If you cut a plant at the stem without uprooting it, the plant will grow back. Whatever generational curses you face must be plucked from the root and destroyed. If you know ministers who can assist with this process, I urge you to seek them out.

VULTURES IN THE CHURCH

It saddens me to have to address the issue of vultures in the church. I thought I was finished with this chapter until I was confronted with a situation that compelled me to warn my sisters in Christ about the vultures in the church. The church should be a safe place for those who are weak, broken or vulnerable, but the truth is the church has been infiltrated by those who use position to gain trust and then abuse their power. Those who are not spiritually mature are the easiest targets.

Today, people can get on social media sites with a click of a mouse and they become whoever they want to be. Please don't be deceived by a man who says he's in the church. Just because he is a Bible toting, scripture quoting, suit wearing brother who portrays himself to be deep in the things of God doesn't mean he really is. The same discretion you would use if you met him on the city bus is the same discretion you should use for a man in the church. The Bible warns us that there are false ministers and you will know them by their fruit! Let's examine his fruit. He is impulsive and inconsistent. He operates in a very similar way but usually is not as physical. Do not be so quick to share your story with him. He might be pretending to empathize with you while making plans for how you can best serve him. Do not be bamboozled into becoming his disciple. The Bible says to, "Know those who labor among you." Watch and pray because eventually, you might be repeating the words of Tina Turner, "I was wondering when the old Ike Turner was gonna shows up."

Instead of his genitals, he prefers to rape you with his title, while manipulating scriptures as a means of intimidation! This vulture is very demanding and controlling. He will call you defiant or rebellious for having legitimate concerns about what he says. He will take advantage of your generosity and cause havoc in your personal life, while destroying what he deems a spiritual life. Some titled clergy such as bishops, apostles, evangelists, pastors, teachers, and ministers are sinister church vultures who will pimp your spiritual gifts and leaves no gratitude for God who gave the spiritual gifts to begin with. So, you must learn the character and behavior. These individuals feel a sense of entitlement, taking credit for the work the Lord has done in you. They will fill your head with false beliefs and religious theories that contradict everything that Jesus represents. You can hear the waves of rage, pride and boastfulness in his voice whenever you challenge him. If you are ever alone with him, you will quickly discern his lustful nature.

> A church vulture will pimp your spiritual gifts and leave no gratitude for God who gave the spiritual gifts to begin with.

The spirit of Jezebel does not have a gender! This wolf in sheep's clothing may start off as a mentor, confidant or spiritual covering, but soon he will say something like, "The

Lord said you are my wife." Do not allow your dreams of a white dress to sway your better judgment. You must be able to hear from God for yourself, so pray! If he starts to speak to you in a condescending way and belittling you, ask yourself, "Is this the mind of Christ?" If you are afraid of him in anyway, get away! If you feel like you must walk on eggshells around him or that he could destroy your reputation, something is wrong! Another sign of a church vulture is that he will threaten you with God as if he can sick God on you like a dog. Run, that is bondage and oppression! God does not even control our will. That kind of behavior is not of God, instead it is spiritually draining and damaging! Take your spiritual life just as serious as you should your physical life. Toxicity will taint your anointing!

Let us pray!

> Lord,
> You are my redeemer, and a very present help in times of trouble. I thank you for truth and salvation. Place a hedge of protection around me and my family. Send angels to war on my behalf. Strengthen me, Lord, and increase my faith. I thank you Jesus for sitting at the right hand of God and making intercessions on my behalf. I need you Lord! Show me who I am in you! Give me a way of escape. Create in me a clean heart and renew a right spirit within me. Destroy every yoke of bondage over me. Give me wisdom, knowledge, and understanding. Wash my mind with your Word. Baptize me with the Holy Ghost and fire. Purge from me, anything that does not reflect you. I submit my will to you. Please sever any connections to people who desire to control your will for my life. Help me to trust you. Allow me to know you are with me. Let you glory be revealed through me. In Jesus' Holy name I pray this prayer and seal it with your blood, Jesus. Amen.

BREAK THE CURSE!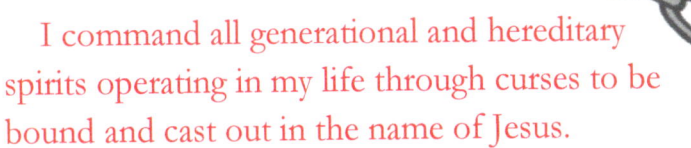

I command all generational and hereditary spirits operating in my life through curses to be bound and cast out in the name of Jesus.

I command all spirits of lust, perversion, adultery, fornication, and immorality to come out of my sexual character, in the name of Jesus.

I command every spirit rooted in bitterness, guilt, shame and condemnation to come out of my conscience, in Jesus' name.

I command all spirits of addiction to come out of my appetite, in Jesus name.

I command all spirits from my past that are hindering my present and future to come out NOW, in Jesus' name!

I command all hidden spirits hiding in any part of my life to come out NOW, in Jesus' name!

I break all curses of premature death and destruction, in Jesus' mighty name!

DYING TO BE LOVED
Chapter Five

Breast implants, buttock injections, alcohol and drugs, cat fights, orgies, being passed around by men and having a same sex love interest is what is being marketed to us every day. Children can barely watch cartoons without seeing images or hearing references of sinful acts. It's important for you not to buy the lie. There is a saying, "If we do not stand for something, we will fall for anything!" It is true that God loves us all. However, just because He loves us doesn't mean He approves of everything we do.

Before the foundation of the Earth, God already knew you. His word says that He knew you before you were even formed in your mother's womb. You had an identity before you were even conceived. The systems of this world want to confuse you and keep you from knowing your true identity which is hidden in Christ.

We were created in His image, yet we search for ourselves through the lens of the media, ignoring our conscience, following every trend and experimenting with things that defile us.

One of the biggest lies we have bought into is, "follow your heart." Listen to what the Bible says about the heart. **Jeremiah 17:9 (KJV)** reveals, *"The heart is deceitful above all things, and desperately wicked: who can know it?"* It is important to understand what love is. Many have reduced love to a feeling.

Love is not an adjective, love is a verb; it's an action word. Love is unconditional. Feelings are based on conditions. Love is patience, it makes sacrifices, and it's not selfish. The biggest act of love is what's described in **John 3:16**, *"For God so loved the world that He gave His only begotten son that whosoever believes in Him, shall not perish but have everlasting life."* He gave his life and that's action; that's love.

We live in a time where matching outfits and being someone's "WCW" (woman crush Wednesday) on Facebook are considered relationship goals. Social media has added new levels of foolishness to relationships that we did not have to contend with before the technology age. People are hooking up easier with random people. They are taking relationship advice from dysfunctional celebrities who are not in healthy relationships. There are leeches, pits, predators, vultures and more lurking in the inboxes of women whose suggestive posts sparks their interest. You can tell a lot about people based on what they post on social media. I have seen females constantly posting sexy photos, but then get upset when guys comment or send them private messages. If you post pictures with revealing cleavage, lingerie, or that focus on your derriere, then expect to get that attention. What respectable woman posts, "I'm horny," for everybody on the Internet to see, then thinks she will get the attention of a man with honorable intentions?

What was once considered honorable and sacred has been reduced to nothing. Loving and honoring one person until God calls them to join Him in Heaven is rejected as something that is old fashion or unattainable. Then there are those who want a wedding but not a marriage. No one wants submission because they have deemed it as weakness. They cannot see its strength. They see a piece of paper, but God sees His covenant. We now embrace any and everything and the line between what is right and wrong is blurred. The lines between good and evil have also been blurred. We have become desensitized to the ills of society while murder, violence, fornication, perversion and illicit behaviors have been glorified. None of these things just happened. I tell people often that the Bible says the devil is a liar, but it does not say he is stupid. The book of Genesis describes him as the most cunning of all. Therefore, we should understand that what we see manifesting now is the result of strategic positioning and influence from the diabolical kingdom. Images and subliminal messages through music and media not only desensitize us to sin but they shape our beliefs. Now, when our favorite actor, basketball player or musician says a certain behavior is okay, it becomes just that.

Ladies, we must stop reinforcing negative emotions, slogans and thought patterns. Whatever you feed will live and whatever you starve will die. How will sitting on your couch with a box of tissue playing the saddest break up songs help you? How will checking his social media pages help you? Stop listening to so-called friends who love dysfunction. Stop torturing yourself. There is nothing therapeutic about pitying yourself, sinking into depression and stressing about a sad situation. Any friend who would encourage you to get intoxicated, fight the other woman or sleep with someone else to get revenge is not a friend. In street terms, "You are playing yourself!" Do not play with your life and health.

Put down your idols. I see those who swear to love Jesus, defend their favorite R&B diva/ artist over the word of God. I heard a song on the radio and the lyrics went something like,

I have too many issues to be a good woman therefore, I do not have the ability to commit and be in a loving, healthy relationship, all I can offer you is good sex. Another more recent song that is charting very well implies in a very catchy, soulful hook that, *even though he physically abuses me, his sex is so good that I cannot get enough.* Why are we sharing Facebook relationship advice post from a woman who once said on her lyrics, "If I had the chance to do it all again, I'll be having sex by the age of 10?" (paraphrasing here). In this day and time it's possible to hear songs that promote the very things that God warns us against and causes us to be blind.

Do you want the yokes of bondage broken off your life? Turn away from sin and idols! You must be deliberate about your deliverance. Saying you are blessed but you're living an oppressed life is an oxymoron! Jesus came that we might have life and have it more abundantly. That's why we must do away with music that glamorizes domestic violence and loose attitudes towards sex. We must turn away from music that lowers our standards and causes us to agree with detestable acts and immoral lifestyles.

To be delivered, you need to be affirmed, encouraged, convicted and transformed. Listen to music that glorifies Jesus! Know God's thoughts toward you! You need to know you are not a failure so do not accept whatever life sends your way. You are more than the poor choices you've made in your past. The past does not determine your destiny. Ask God to send someone who will love you unconditionally. God will redeem the time you lost in bad relationships. Though others have abused or deserted you, your Heavenly Father will never leave you. He has a divine purpose and inheritance for you because you are His child.

Let's pray!

> Father God,
> I come to you in the mighty, matchless name of Jesus Christ, my Savior and redeemer. You are Love! It is my deepest desire to know you. I pray for discernment to recognize what is not from you. Please remove those from my life who do not have my best interest at heart, those who are keeping me from my purpose and who cannot go into this next level of my life. Lord, remove the distractions and help me to live a more disciplined life. I realize that I cannot do this without you. Place the right people in my path who can help me heal and build a stronger relationship with you. Cleanse me of all unrighteousness. Show me your way that I might not stray. Walk with me, Lord, and keep me protected. Create in me a clean heart and renew a right spirit in me. I plead the power of the blood of Jesus over my life. Lord I thank you in advance,
> In Jesus name, Amen.

LET LOVE FIND YOU
Chapter Six

"He who finds a wife finds a good thing and obtains favor from the LORD"- Proverbs 18:22

As a mother, it is vital that I pour into my three sons. I realize that what they learn about womanhood will mostly come from their interactions with me. Recently, I told them that if a woman ever proposes marriage to them, they should say no! They said, "Okay, but why?" I replied, "Because she's too much man for you!" We have allowed social movements to take precedence over divine order. As a result, we have an overall identity crisis taking place, which has caused many negative effects on our households. If we do not turn back to God, generations after generations will be doomed!

I do not totally oppose the feminist movement in its entirety. I agree that pay raises should not be gender specific. I understand that women have career goals and that we live in a time where two incomes are needed to live comfortably. However, I believe that there was a satanic agenda behind this movement and therefore our youth are confused about their roles in relationships. Society no longer acknowledges the traditional feminine role of women and women are appalled at the idea that men should lead the household. Daughters are not being taught how to cook a full course meal and clean a home. Sons are not being taught how to provide and protect.

I don't care what year it is a young lady should not be out working while her man sits on the couch playing the Xbox. She should not be changing a tire while her able-bodied man stands by and watch. Ladies your man should not do a day's work, and then have to go to his mother's house for a home cooked meal.

RENOUNCE AND DENOUNCE

Witchcraft, occults, blood covenants, spells, unnatural affections, pornography, masturbation, orgies, same sex attractions, guilt, shame, condemnation, lying, fornication, adultery, generational curses, rebellion, rejection, depression, fear, anxiety, word curses , poor self-worth, doublemindedness, unforgiveness, idolatry, pride, ego, and rebellion.

AFTERWORD

If you are in an unhealthy relationship, I pray this book has provoked you to rethink your options. Please consider getting the accompanying workbook that includes a variety of activities that will help you further analyze your situation. The workbook also includes an assessment that will help you decide what your next step should be.

I pray you will seek help and make every attempt to keep you and your family safe. Please know there are agencies and others who are waiting to help you. If you can't find a local agency call the **NATIONAL DOMESTIC VIOLENCE HOTLINE:**
800-799-SAFE (7233)

Thank you for reading this book and I pray God will lead, guide, and direct you as you decide what your next step should be. Remember, God will give you the strength to do what you need to do!! Trust Him!

HOW WILL I KNOW ABUSE?
Probing Questions

Twenty-one questions to help you define and recognize what abuse looks like and how to detect if you're in an abusive relationship

1. Are you in a relationship with a person who lies constantly?
2. Are dating someone without disability who depends on you for his basic needs to be met?
3. Are you dating someone who compares you to his other women?
4. Is your relationship causing you to go bankrupt?
5. Does your partner discourage you from pursuing an education or career advancement?
6. Does your partner cheat?
7. Does your partner try to control you?
8. Does your partner verbally, emotionally or physically abuse you?
9. Does your partner blame you for his failures?
10. Does he isolate you from family and friends?
11. Does your partner break up with you without cause and play with your emotions?
12. Has your partner ever manipulated you or forced you to perform a sex act?
13. Are you afraid of your partner?
14. Does your partner spread rumors about you?
15. Does your partner track your phone?
16. Does your partner break or damage your property?
17. Does your partner threaten to harm you, your children, family, friends or pets?

18. Does he humiliate or embarrass you in front of others?
19. Does he use your past against you?
20. Is your partner extremely jealous?
21. Does your partner place false guilt on you or threaten to harm himself if you leave?

> *ANSWERING "YES" TO 2 OR MORE QUESTIONS ARE STRONG INDICATORS THAT YOU NEED TO SEEK HELP AND EXIT THE RELATIONSHIP.*

ABOUT THE AUTHOR

Alicia Shavonn Coleman grew up in the rural small town of Saluda, South Carolina. She struggled academically and behaviorally in school due to childhood trauma. However, Alicia found solace in writing poetry, short stories and scripts for plays. Feeling called to help others in high school she began volunteering at the Special Olympics and tutoring illiterate adults at the Saluda Adult Education program. After graduating from high school, Alicia left the comfort of her hometown to begin her college journey at Benedict College as a first-generation student.

During her college years Alicia became a mother. Becoming a single mother was taxing but she managed to pursue her dreams. Refusing to quit, even after being diagnosed with the neurological disease Gullian Barre' Syndrome, she graduated with a bachelor's degree in social work. Shortly after, Alicia Coleman was licensed by the SC Board of Social Work Examiners. She moved back to her hometown to work with low income families. Aspiring to better serve the marginalized, Alicia enrolled in graduate school. She earned her master's degree in mental health counseling and authored her first book. Shortly after delivering her third child tragedy struck again. Alicia was diagnosed with congestive heart failure but recovered miraculously within a year.

While balancing motherhood and marriage, in 2009 Alicia

answered the calling of ministry. She began doing outreach ministry, hosting conferences, and managing and consulting Christian artists for the Anointed Enterprises Management Company. In 2010, she launched Alicia Coleman Projects, LLC, a social service organization. She provides motivational speaking, assists churches with programs, incorporation, assists non-profit organizations with fundraising and sponsors an Against all Odds academic scholarship for single parents pursuing higher education. Alicia has volunteered at Beyond Abuse, a trauma-based counseling agency that serves sexually abused clients in Greenwood, S.C. She is guardian ad litem in South Carolina and serves as a board member for A Voice for the Children Foundation, Inc. In addition, Alicia is also a therapeutic crisis intervention trainer certified through Cornell University. She is currently employed as a community-based prevention specialist.

For Further Information
www.aliciacprojects.org

AC Projects, LLC
Greenwood, SC 29646
(864) 323-5332

Alicia Coleman
PROJECTS, LLC
est. 2010

www.ingramcontent.com/pod-product-compliance
Lightning Source LLC
Chambersburg PA
CBHW041353290426
44108CB00006B/137